CHANGING COLORS

Work the last stitch to within one step of completion, hook new yarn *(Fig. 5a)* and draw through all loops on hook. Unless otherwise instructed, cut old yarn and work over both ends. When working in rounds, drop old yarn and join with slip stitch to first stitch using new yarn *(Fig. 5b)*.

Fig. 5a

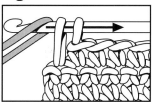

Fig. 5b

FRINGE

Cut a piece of cardboard 3" wide and half as long as fringe specified in individual instructions. Wind the yarn **loosely** and **evenly** around the cardboard lengthwise until the card is filled, then cut across one end; repeat as needed.

Hold together as many strands of yarn as specified in individual instructions; fold in half.

With **wrong** side facing and using a crochet hook, draw the folded end up through a stitch or space and pull the loose ends through the folded end *(Fig. 6a or 6c)*; draw the knot up **tightly** *(Fig. 6b or 6d)*. Repeat, spacing as specified in individual instructions.

Lay flat on a hard surface and trim the ends.

Fig. 6a

Fig. 6b

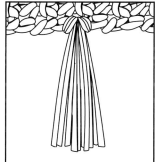

Fig. 6c

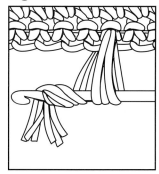

Fig. 6d

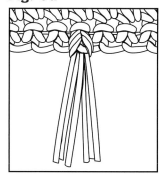

POM-PO

Cut a piece of c
want the diamet
Wind the yarn a.   is
approximately ¹⁄₂" thick in the middle *(Fig. 7a)*.
Carefully slip the yarn off the cardboard and firmly tie an 18" length of yarn around the middle *(Fig. 7b)*. Leave yarn ends long enough to attach the pom-pom. Cut the loops on both ends and trim the pom-pom into a smooth ball *(Fig. 7c)*.

Fig. 7a

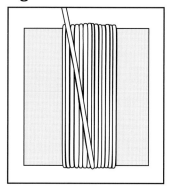

Fig. 7b

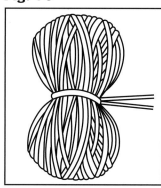

Fig. 7c

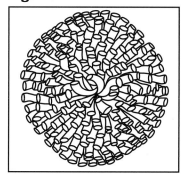

HOW TO MEASURE HEAD

Measure around crown for head measurement *(Fig. 8)*.

Fig. 8

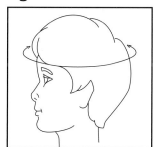

Items made and instructions tested by Cheryl Knepper, Kay Meadors, and Dale Potter.

1. CHILDREN'S TEAM SPIRIT HAT

Hat intended to fit head measurement of approximately 17½" to 21" *(Fig. 8, page 2)*.

MATERIALS
Worsted Weight Yarn:
    Green - 4¾ ounces, (135 grams, 215 yards)
    Yellow - 10 yards
Crochet hook, size G (4.00 mm) **or** size needed for gauge
Afghan hook, size G (4.00 mm) **or** size needed for gauge
Yarn needle

GAUGE: In pattern, 8 sc and 8 rows = 2"

Gauge Swatch: 6⅛"w x 2"h
Work same as Ribbing through Row 8.

STITCH GUIDE

AFGHAN STITCH *(abbreviated Afghan St)*
With yarn in **back**, insert hook from **right** to **left** under next vertical strand *(Fig. 9)*, YO and pull up a loop.

Fig. 9

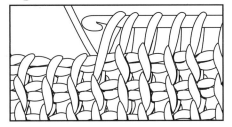

DECREASE
Pull up a loop in next 2 sts, YO and draw through all 3 loops on hook **(counts as one sc)**.

HAT
RIBBING
With crochet hook and Green, ch 25 **loosely**.

Row 1: Sc in second ch from hook and in each ch across: 24 sc.

Rows 2-70: Ch 1, turn; sc in Back Loop Only of each sc across *(Fig. 2, page 1)*; do **not** finish off.

CROWN
Row 1 (Right side)**:** Ch 1, do **not** turn; sc in end of each row across: 70 sc.

Note: Loop a short piece of yarn around any stitch to mark Row 1 as **right** side.

Row 2: Ch 1, turn; sc in first 5 sc, decrease, (sc in next 5 sc, decrease) across: 60 sc.

With **right** side facing, change to afghan hook.

Note: Each Afghan St row is worked in 2 steps, working to the **left** picking up loops and then working to the **right** completing each stitch.

Row 3: Working from **right** to **left**, skip first sc, insert hook in next sc, YO and pull up a loop (2 loops on hook), pull up a loop in each sc across *(Fig. 10a)* (60 loops on hook); working from **left** to **right**, YO and draw through first loop on hook, ★ YO and draw through 2 loops on hook *(Fig. 10b)*; repeat from ★ across until one loop remains on hook. This is the first stitch of the next row.

Fig. 10a

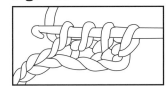

Fig. 10b

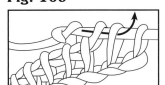

3

Rows 4-9: Working from **right** to **left**, skip first vertical strand, work Afghan Sts across *(Fig. 9, page 3)* (60 loops on hook); working from **left** to **right**, YO and draw through first loop on hook, (YO and draw through 2 loops on hook) across.

Change to crochet hook.

Row 10: Ch 1, do **not** turn; sc in first 4 sts, decrease, (sc in next 4 sts, decrease) across: 50 sc.

Row 11: Ch 1, **turn**; sc in first 3 sc, decrease, (sc in next 3 sc, decrease) across: 40 sc.

Row 12: Ch 1, turn; sc in first 6 sc, decrease, (sc in next 6 sc, decrease) across: 35 sc.

Row 13: Ch 1, turn; sc in first 5 sc, decrease, (sc in next 5 sc, decrease) across: 30 sc.

Row 14: Ch 1, turn; sc in first 4 sc, decrease, (sc in next 4 sc, decrease) across: 25 sc.

Row 15: Ch 1, turn; sc in first 3 sc, decrease, (sc in next 3 sc, decrease) across: 20 sc.

Row 16: Ch 1, turn; sc in first 2 sc, decrease, (sc in next 2 sc, decrease) across: 15 sc.

Row 17: Ch 1, turn; sc in first sc, decrease, (sc in next sc, decrease) across: 10 sc.

Row 18: Ch 1, turn; pull up a loop in first 2 sc, YO and draw through all 3 loops on hook, decrease across; finish off leaving a long end for sewing: 5 sts.

FINISHING
CROSS STITCH

Cross stitch letters on Crown, following Chart and centering words.

Each shaded square on Chart represents one complete cross stitch. Cross stitches are worked over the upright bar of the Afghan St *(Fig. 11)*. If you find it difficult to see where to work the cross stitches, hold the Crown at each side and pull slightly. Evenly spaced holes will be apparent on each side of the upright bars.

Fig. 11

Thread yarn needle with an 18" strand of Yellow. With **right** side of Crown facing, bring needle up from back through first hole, leaving a 3" end on back. Work over this end to secure. Bring needle down through hole diagonally across, pulling yarn flat against Crown, but not so tight as to cause a pucker. You have now made one half of a cross stitch. You can either complete the stitch now, or work across an area in half crosses and then work back, crossing them as you go. Just be sure that the top half of every cross stitch is worked in the same direction.

Finish off by weaving yarn end under several stitches; cut close to work.

Thread yarn needle with yarn end and weave through sts on Row 18 of Crown; gather **tightly**. With **wrong** side together, sew seam.

With Green, make pom-pom *(Figs. 7a-c, page 2)* and sew to top of Hat.

Turn ribbing up.

CHART

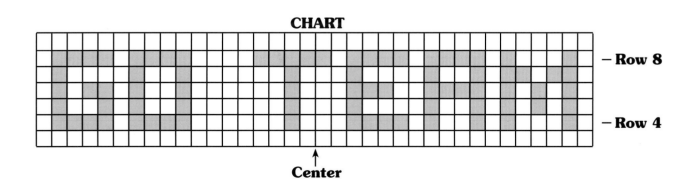

— Row 8

— Row 4

↑
Center

4

2. CHILDREN'S WINTER WARMER SET

Hat intended to fit head measurement of approximately 18½" to 21" *(Fig. 8, page 2)*.

MATERIALS
Worsted Weight Yarn:
   15 ounces, (430 grams, 870 yards)
Crochet hook, size G (4.00 mm) **or** size needed
   for gauge
Yarn needle

GAUGE: In pattern, 16 dc = 4"; 7 rows = 3¾"

Gauge Swatch: 4" square
Ch 18 **loosely**.
Work same as Scarf, page 6, for 7 rows.
Finish off.

STITCH GUIDE

> **FRONT POST DOUBLE CROCHET**
>   *(abbreviated FPdc)*
> YO, insert hook from **front** to **back** around post of st indicated *(Fig. 4, page 1)*, YO and pull up a loop (3 loops on hook), (YO and draw through 2 loops on hook) twice. Skip st behind FPdc.
>
> **FRONT POST TREBLE CROCHET**
>   *(abbreviated FPtr)*
> YO twice, insert hook from **front** to **back** around post of st indicated *(Fig. 4, page 1)*, YO and pull up a loop (4 loops on hook), (YO and draw through 2 loops on hook) 3 times. Skip st behind FPtr.
>
> **BACK POST TREBLE CROCHET**
>   *(abbreviated BPtr)*
> YO twice, insert hook from **back** to **front** around post of st indicated *(Fig. 4, page 1)*, YO and pull up a loop (4 loops on hook), (YO and draw through 2 loops on hook) 3 times. Skip st in front of BPtr.
>
> **BEGINNING SC DECREASE**
> Pull up a loop in first 2 sc, YO and draw through all 3 loops on hook **(counts as one sc)**.
>
> **SC DECREASE**
> Pull up a loop in next 2 sts, YO and draw through all 3 loops on hook **(counts as one sc)**.
>
> **DC DECREASE** (uses next 2 dc)
> ★ YO, insert hook in **next** dc, YO and pull up a loop, YO and draw through 2 loops on hook; repeat from ★ once **more**, YO and draw through all 3 loops on hook **(counts as one dc)**.

HAT
RIBBING
Ch 26 **loosely**.

Row 1 (Wrong side)**:** Dc in fourth ch from hook **(3 skipped chs count as first dc)** and in each ch across: 24 dc.

Note: Loop a short piece of yarn around **back** of any stitch on Row 1 to mark **right** side.

Rows 2-34: Ch 3 **(counts as first dc, now and throughout)**, turn; dc in Back Loop Only of next dc and each dc across *(Fig. 2, page 1)*.

Joining: Ch 1, turn; working in Back Loops Only of dc on Row 34 and in free loops of beginning ch *(Fig. 3b, page 1)*, slip st in each st across; do **not** finish off.

CROWN
Rnd 1: Ch 3, with **right** side facing and working in end of rows, dc in first row, 2 dc in next row and in each row across; join with slip st to first dc: 68 dc.

Rnd 2: Ch 3, **turn**; dc in next dc and in each dc around; join with slip st to first dc.

Rnd 3: Ch 3, turn; work FPtr around dc one rnd **below** next dc, (dc in next 3 dc, work FPtr around dc one rnd **below** next dc) around to last 2 dc, dc in last 2 dc; join with slip st to first dc.

Rnd 4: Ch 3, turn; dc in next 2 dc, work BPtr around next FPtr, (dc in next 3 dc, work BPtr around next FPtr) around; join with slip st to first dc.

Rnd 5: Ch 3, turn; work FPtr around next BPtr, dc decrease, ★ dc in next dc, work FPtr around next BPtr, dc decrease; repeat from ★ around; join with slip st to first dc: 51 sts.

Rnd 6: Ch 3, turn; dc in next dc, work BPtr around next FPtr, (dc in next 2 dc, work BPtr around next FPtr) around; join with slip st to first dc.

Rnd 7: Ch 3, turn; work FPtr around next BPtr, (dc in next 2 dc, work FPtr around next BPtr) around to last dc, dc in last dc; join with slip st to first dc.

Rnd 8: Ch 3, turn; dc in next dc, work BPtr around next FPtr, (dc in next 2 dc, work BPtr around next FPtr) around; join with slip st to first dc.

Rnd 9: Ch 3, turn; work FPtr around next BPtr, (dc decrease, work FPtr around next BPtr) around to last dc, dc in last dc; join with slip st to first dc: 35 sts.

Rnd 10: Ch 3, turn; skip next dc, work BPtr around next FPtr, (dc in next dc, work BPtr around next FPtr) around; join with slip st to first dc: 34 sts.

Rnd 11: Ch 3, turn; work FPdc around next BPtr, (skip next dc, work FPdc around next BPtr) around; join with slip st to first dc, finish off leaving a long end for sewing: 18 sts.

Thread yarn needle with yarn end and weave through sts on Rnd 11 of Crown; gather **tightly** and secure end.

Make pom-pom *(Figs. 7a-c, page 2)* and sew to top of Hat.

Turn ribbing up.

MITTEN (Make 2)
BODY
Ch 35 **loosely**.

Row 1 (Right side)**:** Slip st in second ch from hook and in next ch, hdc in next 22 chs, sc in last 10 chs: 34 sts.

Note #1: Loop a short piece of yarn around any stitch to mark Row 1 as **right** side.

Note #2: Mittens are worked in Back Loops Only throughout *(Fig. 2, page 1)*.

Row 2: Ch 1, turn; sc in first 10 sc, hdc in next 22 hdc, slip st in last 2 slip sts.

Row 3: Turn; slip st in first 2 slip sts, hdc in next 22 hdc, sc in last 10 sc.

Rows 4-19: Repeat Rows 2 and 3, 8 times.

Finish off.

Weave yarn through end of rows at slip st edge and gather **tightly**. With **wrong** side together, working in free loops of beginning ch *(Fig. 3b, page 1)* and in Back Loops Only of sts on Row 19, sew first 12 sts together.

THUMB
FIRST SIDE
Row 1: With **right** side facing, join yarn with sc in first unworked hdc on Row 19 *(see Joining With Sc, page 1)*; sc in next 7 hdc, leave remaining sts unworked: 8 sc.

Row 2: Ch 1, turn; work beginning sc decrease, sc in next 5 sc, 2 sc in last sc.

Row 3: Ch 1, turn; sc in each sc across.

Row 4: Repeat Row 2.

Row 5: Ch 1, turn; sc in first 6 sc, sc decrease: 7 sc.

Row 6: Ch 1, turn; work beginning sc decrease, sc in next 5 sc: 6 sc.

Row 7: Ch 1, turn; work beginning sc decrease, sc in next 2 sc, sc decrease: 4 sc.

Row 8: Ch 1, turn; work beginning sc decrease, sc decrease; finish off: 2 sc.

SECOND SIDE
Row 1: With **wrong** side facing, join yarn with sc in first free loop on beginning ch; sc in next 7 chs, leave remaining chs unworked: 8 sc.

Rows 2-8: Work same as First Side.

Sew Thumb together. Sew remaining sts and chs on Body.

SCARF
Ch 222 **loosely**.

Row 1: Dc in fourth ch from hook **(3 skipped chs count as first dc)** and in each ch across: 220 dc.

Rows 2-13: Ch 3 **(counts as first dc)**, turn; dc in Back Loop Only of next dc and each dc across *(Fig. 2, page 1)*.

Finish off.

Weave yarn through short ends of Scarf; gather **tightly** and secure end.

Make 2 pom-poms *(Figs. 7a-c, page 2)* and sew one pom-pom to each end of Scarf.

3. CHILDREN'S BEAD HAT
Hat intended to fit head measurement of approximately 18½" to 21" *(Fig. 8, page 2)*.

MATERIALS
Worsted Weight Yarn:
4½ ounces, (130 grams, 245 yards)
Crochet hook, size G (4.00 mm) **or** size needed for gauge
Yarn needle
Novelty beads - 17

GAUGE: In pattern, 17 dc and 7 rows = 4"

Gauge Swatch: 4" square
Ch 19 **loosely**.
Row 1: Dc in fourth ch from hook **(3 skipped chs count as first dc)** and in each ch across: 17 dc.
Rows 2-7: Ch 3 **(counts as first dc)**, turn; dc in Back Loop Only of next dc and each dc across *(Fig. 2, page 1)*.
Finish off.

HAT
Ch 65 **loosely**.

Row 1 (Right side)**:** Slip st in second ch from hook and in next 13 chs, sc in next 5 chs, hdc in next 5 chs, dc in next ch and in each ch across: 64 sts.

Note: Loop a short piece of yarn around last dc on Row 1 to mark **right** side and lower edge.

Row 2: Ch 3 **(counts as first dc)**, turn; working in Back Loops Only *(Fig. 2, page 1)*, dc in next 39 dc, hdc in next 5 hdc, sc in next 5 sc, leave remaining sts unworked: 50 sts.

Row 3: Ch 15 **loosely**, turn; slip st in second ch from hook and in next 13 chs, working in Back Loops Only, sc in next 5 sc, hdc in next 5 hdc, dc in next dc and in each dc across: 64 sts.

Rows 4-34: Repeat Rows 2 and 3, 15 times; then repeat Row 2 once **more**.

Finish off, leaving a long end for sewing.

Thread yarn needle with yarn end and weave through end of each row across top of Hat, leaving slip st chs free; gather **tightly**. With **wrong** side together, working in free loops of beginning ch *(Fig. 3b, page 1)* and in Back Loops Only of sts on Row 34, sew Hat together.

Slip bead onto slip st ch; knot end of ch. Slide bead against knot. Repeat for remaining beads.

Roll up bottom edge as desired.

6

4. CHILDREN'S HAT & MITTEN SET

Hat intended to fit head measurement of approximately 18½" to 21" *(Fig. 8, page 2)*.

MATERIALS
Worsted Weight Yarn:
Navy - 3 ounces, (90 grams, 170 yards)
Red - 2 ounces, (60 grams, 115 yards)
White - 1½ ounces, (40 grams, 85 yards)
Crochet hook, size H (5.00 mm) **or** size needed for gauge
Yarn needle

GAUGE: In pattern, 14 sts = 4"; 6 rows = 3¾"

Gauge Swatch: 4" square
Ch 16 **loosely**.
Row 1: Dc in back ridge of fourth ch from hook *(Fig. 1, page 1)* and each ch across **(3 skipped chs count as first dc)**: 14 dc.
Rows 2-6: Ch 3 **(counts as first dc)**, turn; dc in horizontal ridge of next dc and each dc across *(Fig. 13)*. Finish off.

STITCH GUIDE

SC IN HORIZONTAL RIDGE OF SC
Insert hook from **bottom** to **top** in horizontal ridge of next sc *(Fig. 12)*, YO and pull up a loop, YO and draw through both loops on hook.

Fig. 12

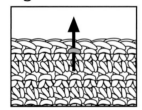

DC IN HORIZONTAL RIDGE OF DC
YO, insert hook from **bottom** to **top** in horizontal ridge of next dc *(Fig. 13)*, YO and pull up a loop (3 loops on hook), (YO and draw through 2 loops on hook) twice.

Fig. 13

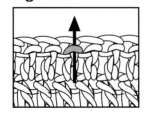

HAT
With Red, ch 42 **loosely**.

Row 1 (Right side)**:** Working in back ridges of beginning ch *(Fig. 1, page 1)*, slip st in second ch from hook and in next ch, sc in next 3 chs, dc in last 36 chs changing to White in last dc *(Fig. 5a, page 2)*: 41 sts.

Note #1: Loop a short piece of yarn around any stitch to mark Row 1 as **right** side.

Note #2: Work in horizontal ridge of each st throughout *(Figs. 12 and 13)* unless otherwise instructed.

Row 2: Ch 3 **(counts as first dc, now and throughout)**, turn; dc in next 35 dc, sc in next 3 sc, slip st in Front Loop Only of last 2 slip sts *(Fig. 2, page 1)* changing to Red in last slip st.

Row 3: Ch 1, turn; slip st in Front Loop Only of first 2 slip sts, sc in next 3 sc, dc in last 36 dc changing to White in last dc.

Row 4: Ch 3, turn; dc in next 35 dc, sc in next 3 sc, slip st in Front Loop Only of last 2 slip sts changing to Red in last slip st.

Row 5: Ch 1, turn; slip st in Front Loop Only of first 2 slip sts, sc in next 3 sc, dc in last 36 dc changing to Navy in last dc.

Row 6: Ch 3, turn; dc in next 35 dc, sc in next 3 sc, slip st in Front Loop Only of last 2 slip sts.

Row 7: Ch 1, turn; slip st in Front Loop Only of first 2 slip sts, sc in next 3 sc, dc in last 36 dc.

Row 8: Ch 3, turn; dc in next 35 dc, sc in next 3 sc, slip st in Front Loop Only of last 2 slip sts changing to Red in last slip st.

Rows 9-12: Repeat Rows 3 and 4 twice.

Rows 13-32: Repeat Rows 5-12 twice, then repeat Rows 5-8 once **more**; at end of Row 32, do **not** change colors, finish off leaving a long end for sewing.

Thread yarn needle with yarn end and weave through slip sts across end of rows; gather **tightly** and secure end. With **wrong** side together, matching sts and working in free loops of beginning ch *(Fig. 3b, page 1)* and in **both** loops of sts on Row 32, sew Hat together.

With Navy, make pom-pom *(Figs. 7a-c, page 2)* and sew to top of Hat.

Roll up bottom edge as desired.

RIGHT MITTEN
BODY
With Navy, ch 29 **loosely**.

Row 1 (Right side)**:** Working in back ridges of beginning ch *(Fig. 1, page 1)*, slip st in second ch from hook, sc in next ch, dc in next 20 chs, sc in last 6 chs: 28 sts.

Note #1: Loop a short piece of yarn around any stitch to mark Row 1 as **right** side.

Note #2: Work in horizontal ridge of each st throughout *(Figs. 12 and 13, page 7)* unless otherwise instructed.

Row 2: Ch 1, turn; sc in Back Loop Only of first 6 sc *(Fig. 2, page 1)* changing to Red in last sc made *(Fig. 5a, page 2)*, do **not** cut Navy, dc in next 20 dc, sc in next sc, slip st in Front Loop Only of last slip st changing to White.

Row 3: Ch 1, turn; slip st in Front Loop Only of first slip st, sc in next sc, dc in next 20 dc changing to Navy in last dc made, sc in Back Loop Only of last 6 sc.

Rows 4 and 5: Repeat Rows 2 and 3.

Row 6: Ch 1, turn; sc in Back Loop Only of first 6 sc changing to Red in last sc made, dc in next 20 dc, sc in next sc, slip st in Front Loop Only of last slip st changing to Navy.

Row 7: Ch 1, turn; slip st in Front Loop Only of first slip st, sc in next sc, dc in next 20 dc, sc in Back Loop Only of last 6 sc.

Row 8: Ch 1, turn; sc in Back Loop Only of first 6 sc, dc in next 20 dc, sc in next sc, slip st in Front Loop Only of last slip st changing to Red.

Row 9: Ch 1, turn; slip st in Front Loop Only of first slip st, sc in next sc, dc in next 20 dc changing to Navy in last dc made, sc in Back Loop Only of last 6 sc.

Row 10: Ch 1, turn; sc in Back Loop Only of first 6 sc changing to White in last sc made, do **not** cut Navy, dc in next 20 dc, sc in next sc, slip st in Front Loop Only of last slip st changing to Red.

Rows 11-13: Repeat Rows 9 and 10 once, then repeat Row 9 once **more**.

Row 14: Ch 1, turn; sc in Back Loop Only of first 6 sc, dc in next 20 dc, sc in next sc, slip st in Front Loop Only of last slip st; finish off leaving a long end for sewing.

Thread yarn needle with yarn end and weave through sts across end of rows; gather **tightly** and secure end. With **wrong** side together, working in free loops of beginning ch *(Fig. 3b, page 1)* and in **both** loops of sts on Row 14, sew first 12 sts. Skip next 8 sts for Thumb opening and sew last 8 sts.

THUMB
Note: Thumb is worked in both loops of each st and in continuous rounds. Do **not** join rounds. Place a 2" scrap piece of yarn before the first stitch of each round, moving marker after each round is complete.

With Navy, ch 3 **loosely**; being careful not to twist ch, join with slip st to form a ring.

Rnd 1 (Right side)**:** Ch 1, 2 sc in each ch around: 6 sc.

Note: Mark Rnd 1 as **right** side.

Rnd 2: 2 Sc in each of next 2 sc, sc in next 4 sc: 8 sc.

Rnd 3: Sc in each sc around.

Rnd 4: 2 Sc in each of next 2 sc, sc in next 6 sc: 10 sc.

Rnd 5: Sc in each sc around.

Rnd 6: 2 Sc in each of next 2 sc, sc in next 8 sc: 12 sc.

Rnd 7: Sc in each sc around.

Rnd 8: 2 Sc in each of next 2 sc, sc in next 10 sc: 14 sc.

Rnd 9: Sc in each sc around.

Rnd 10: 2 Sc in each of next 2 sc, sc in next 12 sc; slip st in next sc, finish off leaving a long end for sewing: 16 sc.

With **right** sides facing, sew Thumb in opening.

LEFT MITTEN
Marking Row 2 of Body as **right** side, work same as Right Mitten.

5. CHILDREN'S EARMUFF

Finished Measurement (excluding ties): 4" x 17½"

MATERIALS
Worsted Weight Yarn:
2½ ounces, (70 grams, 120 yards)
Crochet hook, size I (5.50 mm) **or** size needed
for gauge

GAUGE: In pattern, 6 sts and 7 rows = 2"

Gauge Swatch: 2¼"w (at widest point) x 2"h
Work same as Earmuff through Row 7.

STITCH GUIDE

LOOP STITCH *(abbreviated Loop St)*
(uses one sc)
Insert hook in st indicated, wrap yarn around index
finger of left hand 2 times **more**, insert hook
through all loops on finger following direction
indicated by arrow *(Fig. 14a)*, being careful to hook
all loops *(Fig. 14b)*, draw through st pulling each
loop to measure approximately 1½", remove finger
from loops, YO and draw through all 4 loops on
hook **(Loop St made,** *Fig. 14c)*.

Fig. 14a

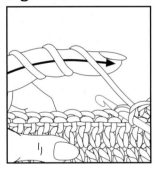

Fig. 14b

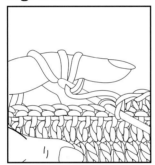

Fig. 14c

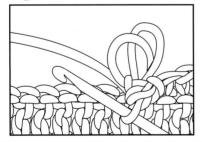

EARMUFF

Row 1: Ch 3, work Loop St in second ch from hook
and in next ch *(Figs. 14a-c)*.

Row 2 (Right side)**:** Ch 1, turn; 2 sc in each st across:
4 sc.

Row 3: Ch 1, turn; work Loop St in each sc across.

Row 4: Ch 1, turn; 2 sc in first st, sc in each st across to
last st, 2 sc in last st: 6 sc.

Rows 5-11: Repeat Rows 3 and 4, 3 times; then
repeat Row 3 once **more**: 12 Loop Sts.

Row 12: Ch 1, turn; sc in each st across.

Row 13: Ch 1, turn; work Loop St in each sc across.

Rows 14-51: Repeat Rows 12 and 13, 19 times.

Row 52: Ch 1, turn; pull up a loop in first 2 sts, YO
and draw through all 3 loops on hook, sc in each st
across to last 2 sts, pull up a loop in last 2 sts, YO and
draw through all 3 loops on hook: 10 sts.

Row 53: Ch 1, turn; work Loop St in each st across.

Rows 54-59: Repeat Rows 52 and 53, 3 times:
4 Loop Sts.

Row 60: Ch 1, turn; pull up a loop in first 2 sts, YO
and draw through all 3 loops on hook, pull up a loop
in last 2 sts, YO and draw through all 3 loops on hook:
2 sts.

Row 61: Ch 1, turn; work Loop St in each st across; do
not finish off.

EDGING AND TIES
Ch 1, turn; sc in first Loop St, ch 51 **loosely**, slip st in
second ch from hook and in each ch across, sc in next
Loop St; sc in end of each row across; working in free
loops of beginning ch *(Fig. 3b, page 1)*, sc in first ch,
ch 51 **loosely**, slip st in second ch from hook and in
each ch across, sc in last free loop; sc in end of each row
across; join with slip st to first sc, finish off.

6

5

4

11

3

7

2

8

9

1

6. CHILDREN'S HOODED SCARF

Hood intended to fit head measurement of approximately 18½" to 21" *(Fig. 8, page 2)*.

MATERIALS

Worsted Weight Yarn:
Red - 4¾ ounces, (135 grams, 270 yards)
White - 3 ounces, (90 grams, 170 yards)
Crochet hook, size I (5.50 mm) **or** size needed for gauge
Yarn needle

GAUGE: In pattern, two repeats = 3¼";
5 rows = 3"

Gauge Swatch: 4" square
Ch 16 **loosely**.
Work same as Scarf for 7 rows.

STITCH GUIDE

CLUSTER (uses next 5 sts)
★ YO, insert hook in **next** st, YO and pull up a loop, YO and draw through 2 loops on hook; repeat from ★ 4 times **more**, YO and draw through all 6 loops on hook.

HOOD

With Red, ch 37 **loosely**.

Row 1 (Right side)**:** 2 Dc in fourth ch from hook **(3 skipped chs count as first dc)**, skip next 2 chs, sc in next ch, ★ skip next 2 chs, 5 dc in next ch, skip next 2 chs, sc in next ch; repeat from ★ across; working in free loops of beginning ch *(Fig. 3b, page 1)*, (5 dc in ch at base of next 5-dc group, sc in ch at base of next sc) 5 times, skip next 2 chs, 3 dc in next ch; do **not** join, finish off: 67 sts.

Note: Loop a short piece of yarn around any stitch to mark Row 1 as **right** side.

Row 2: With **wrong** side facing, join White with sc in first dc *(see Joining With Sc, page 1)*; ★ ch 2, work Cluster, ch 2, sc in next dc; repeat from ★ across; finish off: 12 sc and 11 Clusters.

Row 3: With **right** side facing, join Red with slip st in first sc; ch 3 **(counts as first dc, now and throughout)**, 2 dc in same st, sc in next Cluster, (5 dc in next sc, sc in next Cluster) across to last sc, 3 dc in last sc; finish off: 67 sts.

Rows 4-17: Repeat Rows 2 and 3, 7 times.

SCARF

With Red, ch 58 **loosely**; with **wrong** side of Hood facing, work 72 sc evenly spaced across end of rows, ch 60 **loosely**: 72 sc and 118 chs.

Row 1: 2 Dc in fourth ch from hook **(3 skipped chs count as first dc)**, skip next 2 chs, sc in next ch, ★ skip next 2 sts, 5 dc in next st, skip next 2 sts, sc in next st; repeat from ★ across to last 3 chs, skip next 2 chs, 3 dc in last ch; finish off: 187 sts.

Row 2: With **wrong** side facing, join White with sc in first dc; ★ ch 2, work Cluster, ch 2, sc in next dc; repeat from ★ across; finish off: 32 sc and 31 Clusters.

Row 3: With **right** side facing, join Red with slip st in first sc; ch 3, 2 dc in same st, sc in next Cluster, (5 dc in next sc, sc in next Cluster) across to last sc, 3 dc in last sc; finish off: 187 sts.

Rows 4-7: Repeat Rows 2 and 3 twice.

TASSEL

Cut a piece of cardboard 3" wide and 9" long. Wind a double strand of Red yarn around the cardboard lengthwise approximately 36 times. Cut an 18" length of yarn and insert it under all of the strands at the top of the cardboard; pull up **tightly** and tie securely. Leave the yarn ends long enough to attach the tassel. Cut the yarn at the opposite end of the cardboard and then remove it *(Fig. 15a)*. Cut a 6" length of yarn and wrap it **tightly** around the tassel twice, 1" below the top *(Fig. 15b)*; tie securely. Trim the ends.

Sew tassel to top point of Hood.

Fig. 15a

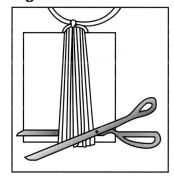

Fig. 15b

Holding 7 strands of Red together, each 12" long, add fringe in every other row across short ends of Scarf *(Figs. 6a & b, page 2)*.

14

7. CHILDREN'S FLOWER HAT

Hat intended to fit head measurement of approximately 18½" to 21" *(Fig. 8, page 2)*.

MATERIALS
Worsted Weight Yarn:
 Navy - 2¼ ounces, (65 grams, 140 yards)
 Lavender - ½ ounce, (20 grams, 30 yards)
 Pink - ½ ounce, (20 grams, 30 yards)
 Purple - ½ ounce, (20 grams, 30 yards)
 Green - 6 yards
Crochet hooks, sizes F (3.75 mm) **and** I (5.50 mm)
 or sizes needed for gauge
Yarn needle

GAUGE SWATCH
Hat - 3" diameter
Work same as Hat through Rnd 3.

Flower - 1½" diameter
Work same as Center.

HAT
With Navy and using large size hook, ch 3; join with slip st to form a ring.

Rnd 1 (Right side)**:** Ch 2 **(counts as first hdc, now and throughout)**, 11 hdc in ring; join with slip st to first hdc: 12 hdc.

Note: Loop a short piece of yarn around any stitch to mark Rnd 1 as **right** side.

Rnd 2: Ch 2, hdc in sp **before** next hdc, 2 hdc in sp **before** each hdc around; join with slip st to first hdc: 24 hdc.

Rnd 3: Ch 2, hdc in sp **before** each of next 2 hdc, 2 hdc in sp **before** next hdc, ★ hdc in sp **before** each of next 3 hdc, 2 hdc in sp **before** next hdc; repeat from ★ around; join with slip st to first hdc: 30 hdc.

Rnd 4: Ch 2, hdc in sp **before** each of next 3 hdc, 2 hdc in sp **before** next hdc, ★ hdc in sp **before** each of next 4 hdc, 2 hdc in sp **before** next hdc; repeat from ★ around; join with slip st to first hdc: 36 hdc.

Rnd 5: Ch 2, hdc in sp **before** each of next 4 hdc, 2 hdc in sp **before** next hdc, ★ hdc in sp **before** each of next 5 hdc, 2 hdc in sp **before** next hdc; repeat from ★ around; join with slip st to first hdc: 42 hdc.

Rnd 6: Ch 2, hdc in sp **before** each of next 5 hdc, 2 hdc in sp **before** next hdc, ★ hdc in sp **before** each of next 6 hdc, 2 hdc in sp **before** next hdc; repeat from ★ around; join with slip st to first hdc: 48 hdc.

Rnd 7: Ch 2, hdc in sp **before** each of next 6 hdc, 2 hdc in sp **before** next hdc, ★ hdc in sp **before** each of next 7 hdc, 2 hdc in sp **before** next hdc; repeat from ★ around; join with slip st to first hdc: 54 hdc.

Rnd 8: Ch 2, hdc in sp **before** each of next 7 hdc, 2 hdc in sp **before** next hdc, ★ hdc in sp **before** each of next 8 hdc, 2 hdc in sp **before** next hdc; repeat from ★ around; join with slip st to first hdc: 60 hdc.

Rnds 9-16: Ch 2, hdc in sp **before** each hdc around; join with slip st to first hdc.

Rnd 17: Ch 1, sc in sp **before** each hdc around; join with slip st to first sc.

Rnds 18-21: Ch 1, sc in same st and in each sc around; join with slip st to first sc.

Finish off.

FLOWER (Make 3)
Note: Make one **each** of Lavender, Pink, and Purple.

CENTER
Rnd 1 (Right side)**:** With color indicated and using small size hook, ch 2, 6 sc in second ch from hook; do **not** join, place marker.

Note #1: Loop a short piece of yarn around any stitch to mark Rnd 1 as **right** side.

Note #2: Do **not** join rounds. Place a 2" scrap piece of yarn before the first stitch of each round, moving marker after each round is complete.

Rnd 2: 2 Sc in Back Loop Only of each sc around *(Fig. 2, page 1)*: 12 sc.

Rnd 3: Working in Back Loops Only, (2 sc in next sc, sc in next sc) around; slip st in next sc, finish off leaving a long end for sewing: 18 sc.

PETALS
With **right** side facing, using small size hook, and working in free loops of Rnds 1 and 2 *(Fig. 3a, page 1)* and in Front Loops Only of sc on Rnd 3, join same color yarn with slip st in first sc on Rnd 1; (ch 3, 3 dc, ch 3, slip st) in same st, (slip st, ch 3, 3 dc, ch 3, slip st) in each sc around; finish off.

LEAF (Make 2)
With Green and using small size hook, ch 10 **loosely**; 2 dc in fourth ch from hook and in next ch, hdc in next 2 chs, sc in next 2 chs, (slip st, ch 2, slip st) in last ch; working in free loops of beginning ch *(Fig. 3b, page 1)*, sc in next 2 chs, hdc in next 2 chs, 2 dc in each of next 2 chs; join with slip st to top of beginning ch, finish off.

Using photo as a guide for placement, sew Flowers and Leaves to Hat.

8. CHILDREN'S HEADBAND

Headband intended to fit head measurement of approximately 18½" to 21" (*Fig. 8, page 2*).

MATERIALS
Worsted Weight Yarn:
1¼ ounces, (35 grams, 70 yards)
Crochet hook, size G (4.00 mm) **or** size needed for gauge
Yarn needle

GAUGE: In pattern, 8 sts and 5 rows = 2"

Gauge Swatch: 2" square
Ch 10 **loosely**.
Work same as Headband.

STITCH GUIDE

> **FRONT POST DOUBLE CROCHET**
> **(abbreviated FPdc)**
> YO, insert hook from **front** to **back** around post of st indicated (*Fig. 4, page 1*), YO and pull up a loop (3 loops on hook), (YO and draw through 2 loops on hook) twice. Skip st behind FPdc.
>
> **BACK POST DOUBLE CROCHET**
> **(abbreviated BPdc)**
> YO, insert hook from **back** to **front** around post of st indicated (*Fig. 4, page 1*), YO and pull up a loop (3 loops on hook), (YO and draw through 2 loops on hook) twice. Skip st in front of BPdc.

HEADBAND
Ch 74 **loosely**.

Row 1 (Right side): Dc in back ridge of fourth ch from hook (*Fig. 1, page 1*) and each ch across (**3 skipped chs count as first dc**): 72 dc.

Row 2: Ch 3 **(counts as first dc, now and throughout)**, turn; (work FPdc around next dc, work BPdc around next dc) across to last dc, dc in last dc.

Rows 3-5: Ch 3, turn; (work FPdc around next BPdc, work BPdc around next FPdc) across to last dc, dc in last dc.

Finish off, leaving a long end for sewing.

Thread yarn needle with yarn end and sew ends of Headband together.

9. ADULTS' HAT

MATERIALS
Worsted Weight Yarn:
5½ ounces, (160 grams, 300 yards)
Crochet hook, size J (6.00 mm) **or** size needed for gauge

Note: Hat is worked holding two strands of yarn together.

GAUGE SWATCH: 4" diameter
Work same as Hat through Rnd 2.

HAT
Ch 3; join with slip st to form a ring.

Rnd 1 (Right side): Ch 3 **(counts as first dc, now and throughout)**, 11 dc in ring; join with slip st to first dc: 12 dc.

Rnd 2: Slip st in sp **before** next dc, ch 3, dc in same sp, 2 dc in sp **before** each dc around; join with slip st to first dc: 24 dc.

Rnd 3: Slip st in sp **before** next dc, ch 3, dc in sp **before** each of next 2 dc, 2 dc in sp **before** next dc, ★ dc in sp **before** each of next 3 dc, 2 dc in sp **before** next dc; repeat from ★ around; join with slip st to first dc: 30 dc.

Rnd 4: Slip st in sp **before** next dc, ch 3, dc in sp **before** each of next 3 dc, 2 dc in sp **before** next dc, ★ dc in sp **before** each of next 4 dc, 2 dc in sp **before** next dc; repeat from ★ around; join with slip st to first dc: 36 dc.

Rnd 5: Slip st in sp **before** next dc, ch 3, dc in sp **before** each dc around; join with slip st to first dc.

Rnd 6: Slip st in sp **before** next dc, ch 3, dc in sp **before** each of next 4 dc, 2 dc in sp **before** next dc, ★ dc in sp **before** each of next 5 dc, 2 dc in sp **before** next dc; repeat from ★ around; join with slip st to first dc: 42 dc.

Rnd 7: Slip st in sp **before** next dc, ch 3, dc in sp **before** each dc around; join with slip st to first dc.

Rnd 8: Slip st in sp **before** next dc, ch 3, dc in sp **before** each of next 5 dc, 2 dc in sp **before** next dc, ★ dc in sp **before** each of next 6 dc, 2 dc in sp **before** next dc; repeat from ★ around; join with slip st to first dc: 48 dc.

Rnds 9-16: Slip st in sp **before** next dc, ch 3, dc in sp **before** each dc around; join with slip st to first dc.

Rnd 17: Ch 1, sc in sp **before** each dc around; join with slip st to first sc, finish off.

Roll up bottom edge as desired.

10. ADULTS' HAT & MUFF SET

MATERIALS
Worsted Weight Yarn:
9¾ ounces, (280 grams, 550 yards)
Crochet hook, size I (5.50 mm) **or** size needed for gauge
Faux fur fabric - ½ yard
Sewing needle and thread
Yarn needle
Polyester fiberfill

Note: Hat and Muff Set is worked holding two strands of yarn together.

GAUGE SWATCH: 3½" diameter
Work same as Hat through Rnd 2.

STITCH GUIDE

> **DECREASE**
> Pull up a loop in next 2 sc, YO and draw through all 3 loops on hook **(counts as one sc)**.

HAT
Ch 3; join with slip st to form a ring.

Rnd 1 (Right side)**:** Ch 3 **(counts as first dc, now and throughout)**, 11 dc in ring; join with slip st to first dc: 12 dc.

Note: Loop a short piece of yarn around any stitch to mark Rnd 1 as **right** side.

Rnd 2: Ch 3, dc in same st, 2 dc in next dc and in each dc around; join with slip st to first dc: 24 dc.

Rnd 3: Ch 3, 2 dc in next dc, (dc in next dc, 2 dc in next dc) around; join with slip st to first dc: 36 dc.

Rnd 4: Ch 3, dc in next 2 dc, 2 dc in next dc, (dc in next 3 dc, 2 dc in next dc) around; join with slip st to first dc: 45 dc.

Rnd 5: Ch 3, dc in next 3 dc, 2 dc in next dc, (dc in next 4 dc, 2 dc in next dc) around; join with slip st to first dc: 54 dc.

Rnds 6-8: Ch 3, dc in next dc and in each dc around; join with slip st to first dc.

Rnds 9 and 10: Ch 1, sc in same st and in each st around; join with slip st to first sc.

Finish off.

TRIM
Cut one piece of fabric 6" x 33½". With **right** side together and using a ¼" seam allowance, sew long edge of fabric together. Turn right side out and stuff lightly with polyester fiberfill. Turn raw edges to inside and sew short edges together forming a tube.

Sew Trim to Rnd 10 with seam at back of Hat.

MUFF
Ch 30 **loosely**; being careful not to twist ch, join with slip st to form a ring.

Rnd 1 (Right side)**:** Ch 3 **(counts as first dc, now and throughout)**, dc in next ch and in each ch around; join with slip st to first dc: 30 dc.

Note: Loop a short piece of yarn around any stitch to mark Rnd 1 as **right** side.

Rnds 2-12: Ch 3, dc in next dc and in each dc around; join with slip st to first dc.

Note: Do **not** join remaining rounds. Place a 2" scrap piece of yarn before the first stitch of each round, moving marker after each round is complete.

Rnd 13: Ch 1, working in Back Loops Only *(Fig. 2, page 1)*, sc in same st and in next dc, 2 sc in next dc, (sc in next 2 dc, 2 sc in next dc) around: 40 sc.

Rnd 14: Working in both loops, (sc in next 3 sc, 2 sc in next sc) around: 50 sc.

Rnds 15-37: Sc in each sc around.

Rnd 38: (Sc in next 3 sc, decrease) around: 40 sc.

Rnd 39: (Sc in next 2 sc, decrease) around; slip st in next sc, finish off: 30 sc.

ASSEMBLY
With **wrong** side together, working in free loops of beginning ch *(Fig. 3b, page 1)* and in Back Loops Only of sts on Rnd 39, sew Muff together, stuffing polyester fiberfill between layers of folded Muff to desired firmness before closing.

TRIM
Cut two pieces of fabric 6" x 27½" each. Complete same as Hat Trim. Sew Trim to each end of Muff.

11. ADULTS' SCARF

Finished Size: 6" x 57"

MATERIALS

Worsted Weight Yarn:
5¾ ounces, (165 grams, 325 yards)
Crochet hook, size H (5.00 mm) **or** size needed for gauge

GAUGE: In pattern, 11 dc and 7 rows = 3"

Gauge Swatch: 4¼"w x 3"h
Ch 16 **loosely**.
Work same as Scarf for 7 rows.
Finish off.

STITCH GUIDE

> **PUFF STITCH** *(abbreviated Puff St)*
> ★ YO, insert hook in dc indicated, YO and pull up a loop; repeat from ★ 2 times **more**, YO and draw through all 7 loops on hook.

SCARF

Ch 208 **loosely**.

Row 1 (Right side)**:** Sc in back ridge of second ch from hook *(Fig. 1, page 1)* and each ch across: 207 sc.

Note: Loop a short piece of yarn around any stitch to mark Row 1 as **right** side.

Row 2: Ch 3 **(counts as first dc)**, turn; dc in next sc and in each sc across.

Row 3: Ch 1, turn; sc in first 2 dc, ch 3, skip next 2 dc, work Puff St in next dc, ch 3, ★ skip next 2 dc, sc in next dc, ch 3, skip next 2 dc, work Puff St in next dc, ch 3; repeat from ★ across to last 4 dc, skip next 2 dc, sc in last 2 dc: 34 Puff Sts.

Row 4: Ch 5 **(counts as first dc plus ch 2)**, turn; skip next sc, 3 sc in next Puff St, (ch 3, 3 sc in next Puff St) across to last 2 sc, ch 2, skip next sc, dc in last sc: 104 sts and 35 sps.

Row 5: Ch 1, turn; sc in first dc, 2 sc in next ch-2 sp, sc in next 3 sc, (3 sc in next ch-3 sp, sc in next 3 sc) across to last ch-2 sp, 2 sc in last ch-2 sp, sc in last dc: 207 sc.

Rows 6-14: Repeat Rows 2-5 twice, then repeat Row 2 once **more**.

Row 15: Ch 1, turn; sc in each dc across; finish off.

Holding 7 strands of yarn together, each 14" long, add fringe in every other row across ends of Scarf *(Figs. 6a & b, page 2)*.

12. ADULTS' HEADBAND

MATERIALS

Worsted Weight Yarn:
2 ounces, (60 grams, 110 yards)
Crochet hook, size H (5.00 mm) **or** size needed for gauge
Yarn needle

GAUGE: In pattern, 14 dc and 6 rows = 4"

Gauge Swatch: 6¾"w x 4"h
Work same as Headband through Row 6.

HEADBAND

Ch 26 **loosely**.

Row 1: Dc in fourth ch from hook **(3 skipped chs count as first dc)** and in each ch across: 24 dc.

Row 2 (Right side)**:** Ch 3 **(counts as first dc, now and throughout)**, turn; dc in Back Loop Only of next dc and each dc across *(Fig. 2, page 1)*.

Note: Loop a short piece of yarn around any stitch to mark Row 2 as **right** side.

Row 3: Ch 3, turn; dc in Front Loop Only of next dc and each dc across.

Row 4: Ch 3, turn; dc in Back Loop Only of next dc and each dc across.

Rows 5-32: Repeat Rows 3 and 4, 14 times.

Finish off, leaving a long end for sewing.

Thread yarn needle with yarn end. With **wrong** side together, working in free loops of beginning ch *(Fig. 3b, page 1)* and in Back Loops Only of sts on Row 32, sew seam. With **wrong** side together, sew end of rows together. Roll seam to inside of Headband.

13. ADULTS' NECK WRAP

Finished Size: 5¾" x 33"

MATERIALS
Worsted Weight Yarn:
3¼ ounces, (95 grams, 200 yards)
Crochet hook, size H (5.00 mm) **or** size needed for gauge

GAUGE: In pattern, (Cluster, ch 1) 8 times = 4½";
5 rows = 3¼"

Gauge Swatch: 4½"w x 2"h
Ch 19 **loosely**.
Work same as Neck Wrap for 3 rows.
Finish off.

STITCH GUIDE

> **BEGINNING CLUSTER**
> YO, insert hook in same st, YO and pull up a loop, YO and draw through 2 loops on hook, YO, skip next ch, insert hook in next st, YO and pull up a loop, YO and draw through 2 loops on hook, YO and draw through all 3 loops on hook.
>
> **CLUSTER**
> YO, insert hook in same st as last st made, YO and pull up a loop, YO and draw through 2 loops on hook, YO, skip next ch, insert hook in next st, YO and pull up a loop, YO and draw through 2 loops on hook, YO and draw through all 3 loops on hook.

NECK WRAP
Ch 123 **loosely**.

Row 1 (Right side)**:** YO, insert hook in fourth ch from hook **(3 skipped chs count as first dc)**, YO and pull up a loop, YO and draw through 2 loops on hook, YO, skip next ch, insert hook in next ch, YO and pull up a loop, YO and draw through 2 loops on hook, YO and draw through all 3 loops on hook, ch 1, (work Cluster, ch 1) across to last ch, dc in last ch: 61 sts and 59 ch-1 sps.

Note: Loop a short piece of yarn around any stitch to mark Row 1 as **right** side.

Rows 2-4: Ch 3 **(counts as first dc, now and throughout)**, turn; work Beginning Cluster, ch 1, (work Cluster, ch 1) across to last dc, dc in last dc.

Row 5: Ch 3, turn; work Beginning Cluster, ch 1, (work Cluster, ch 1) 43 times, dc in same st as last st made, ch 13 **loosely**, skip next 6 Clusters, dc in next Cluster, ch 1, (work Cluster, ch 1) across to last dc, dc in last dc: 52 Clusters and 4 dc.

Rows 6-9: Ch 3, turn; work Beginning Cluster, ch 1, (work Cluster, ch 1) across to last dc, dc in last dc: 59 Clusters and 2 dc.

Finish off.

TRIM
With **right** side facing, join yarn with sc in first skipped ch on Row 4 *(see Joining With Sc, page 1)*; sc in each Cluster and in each ch across, sc in side of next dc; working in free loops of ch-13 *(Fig. 3b, page 1)*, sc in each ch across, sc in side of next dc; join with slip st to first sc, finish off.

Holding 5 strands of yarn together, each 13" long, add fringe in each row across ends of Neck Wrap *(Figs. 6a & b, page 2)*.

14. ADULTS' STRIPED CAP

MATERIALS
Worsted Weight Yarn:
Dk Grey - 5¾ ounces, (165 grams, 360 yards)
Lt Grey - 1 ounce, (30 grams, 60 yards)
Red - ½ ounce, (20 grams, 30 yards)
Crochet hook, size I (5.50 mm) **or** size needed for gauge
Yarn needle

GAUGE: In pattern, 8 sts and 5 rows = 2"

Gauge Swatch: 2" square
Ch 11 **loosely**.
Work same as Cap for 5 rows.
Finish off.

STITCH GUIDE

> **FRONT POST DOUBLE CROCHET**
> *(abbreviated FPdc)*
> YO, insert hook from **front** to **back** around post of st indicated *(Fig. 4, page 1)*, YO and pull up a loop (3 loops on hook), (YO and draw through 2 loops on hook) twice. Skip st behind FPdc.
>
> **BACK POST DOUBLE CROCHET**
> *(abbreviated BPdc)*
> YO, insert hook from **back** to **front** around post of st indicated *(Fig. 4, page 1)*, YO and pull up a loop (3 loops on hook), (YO and draw through 2 loops on hook) twice. Skip st in front of BPdc.
>
> **DECREASE**
> Pull up a loop in next 2 sts, YO and draw through all 3 loops on hook **(counts as one sc)**.

CAP

With Dk Grey, ch 89 **loosely**.

Row 1: Dc in back ridge of fourth ch from hook *(Fig. 1, page 1)* and each ch across **(3 skipped chs count as first dc)**: 87 dc.

Row 2: Ch 3 **(counts as first dc, now and throughout)**, turn; work BPdc around next dc, (work FPdc around next dc, work BPdc around next dc) across to last dc, dc in last dc.

Row 3: Ch 3, turn; work FPdc around next BPdc, (work BPdc around next FPdc, work FPdc around next BPdc) across to last dc, dc in last dc.

Row 4: Ch 3, turn; work BPdc around next FPdc, (work FPdc around next BPdc, work BPdc around next FPdc) across to last dc, dc in last dc.

Rows 5-7: Repeat Rows 3 and 4 once, then repeat Row 3 once **more**.

Row 8 (Right side)**:** Ch 1, turn; sc in Front Loop Only of each st across *(Fig. 2, page 1)*.

Row 9: Ch 3, turn; dc in both loops of next sc and each sc across.

Row 10: Ch 3, turn; work FPdc around next dc, (work BPdc around next dc, work FPdc around next dc) across to last dc, dc in last dc.

Row 11: Ch 3, turn; work BPdc around next FPdc, (work FPdc around next BPdc, work BPdc around next FPdc) across to last dc, dc in last dc.

Row 12: Ch 3, turn; work FPdc around next BPdc, (work BPdc around next FPdc, work FPdc around next BPdc) across to last dc, dc in last dc.

Rows 13-15: Repeat Rows 11 and 12 once, then repeat Row 11 once **more** changing to Lt Grey in last dc on Row 15 *(Fig. 5a, page 2)*.

Row 16: Repeat Row 12 changing to Red in last dc.

Row 17: Repeat Row 11 changing to Lt Grey in last dc.

Row 18: Repeat Row 12 changing to Dk Grey in last dc.

Rows 19-21: Repeat Rows 11 and 12 once, then repeat Row 11 once **more**.

Row 22: Ch 3, turn; work FPdc around next BPdc, ★ work BPdc around next FPdc, work FPdc around **both** posts of next 2 BPdc (skipping FPdc between), work BPdc around next FPdc, work FPdc around next BPdc; repeat from ★ across to last dc, dc in last dc changing to Lt Grey: 59 sts.

Row 23: Repeat Row 11 changing to Red in last dc.

Row 24: Repeat Row 12 changing to Lt Grey in last dc.

Row 25: Repeat Row 11 changing to Dk Grey in last dc.

Row 26: Repeat Row 12.

Row 27: Repeat Row 11.

Row 28: Ch 3, turn; ★ work FPdc around next BPdc, work BPdc around next FPdc, work FPdc around **both** posts of next 2 BPdc (skipping FPdc between), work BPdc around next FPdc; repeat from ★ across to last 4 sts, work FPdc around **both** posts of next 2 BPdc (skipping FPdc between), dc in last dc: 39 sts.

Row 29: Repeat Row 11.

Row 30: Ch 3, turn; ★ work FPdc around **both** posts of next 2 BPdc (skipping FPdc between), work BPdc around next FPdc; repeat from ★ across to last 2 sts, work FPdc around next BPdc, dc in last dc: 21 sts.

Row 31: Ch 1, turn; pull up a loop in first 3 sts, YO and draw through all 4 loops on hook, decrease across: 10 sts.

Row 32: Ch 1, turn; pull up a loop in first 2 sts, YO and draw through all 3 loops on hook, decrease across; finish off leaving a long end for sewing: 5 sts.

Thread yarn needle with yarn end and weave through sts on Row 32; gather **tightly**. Sew seam.

Turn bottom edge up along Row 7.

15. ADULTS' SKI CAP

MATERIALS
Worsted Weight Yarn:
 Dk Blue - 3½ ounces, (100 grams, 200 yards)
 Blue - 1½ ounces, (40 grams, 85 yards)
Crochet hook, size G (4.00 mm) **or** size needed
 for gauge
Yarn needle

GAUGE: 8 sc and 8 rows = 2"

Gauge Swatch: 7"w x 2"h
Work same as Ribbing through Row 8.

STITCH GUIDE

LONG SINGLE CROCHET *(abbreviated LSC)*
Working **around** next sc, insert hook in sc one
row **below**, YO and pull up a loop even with last
st made, YO and draw through both loops on hook
(Fig. 16) **(counts as one sc)**.

Fig. 16

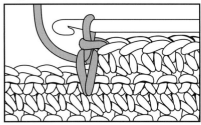

DECREASE
Pull up a loop in next 2 sc, YO and draw through all
3 loops on hook **(counts as one sc)**.

CAP
RIBBING
With Dk Blue, ch 29 **loosely**.

Row 1 (Wrong side)**:** Sc in second ch from hook and in
each ch across: 28 sc.

Note: Loop a short piece of yarn around **back** of any
stitch on Row 1 to mark **right** side.

Rows 2-72: Ch 1, turn; sc in Back Loop Only of each
sc across *(Fig. 2, page 1)*.

Finish off, leaving a long end for sewing.

Thread yarn needle with yarn end. With **wrong** side
together, working in free loops of beginning ch *(Fig. 3b,
page 1)* and in Back Loops Only of sts on Row 72, sew
seam.

CROWN
Rnd 1: With **right** side facing, join Dk Blue with sc
in end of first row *(see Joining With Sc, page 1)*; sc
in end of each row around; join with slip st to first sc
changing to Blue *(Fig. 5b, page 2)*: 72 sc.

Rnd 2: Ch 1, sc in same st and in next sc, decrease, (sc
in next 4 sc, decrease) around to last 2 sc, sc in last 2 sc;
join with slip st to first sc changing to Dk Blue: 60 sc.

Rnd 3: Ch 1, sc in same st and in next 3 sc, work LSC
(Fig. 16), (sc in next 4 sc, work LSC) around; join with
slip st to first sc changing to Blue.

Rnd 4: Ch 1, sc in same st and in each sc around; join
with slip st to first sc changing to Dk Blue.

Rnd 5: Ch 1, sc in same st and in next 3 sc, work LSC,
(sc in next 4 sc, work LSC) around; join with slip st to
first sc changing to Blue.

Rnds 6-8: Ch 1, sc in same st and in each sc around;
join with slip st to first sc.

Rnd 9: Ch 1, sc in same st and in each sc around; join
with slip st to first sc changing to Dk Blue.

Rnd 10: Ch 1, sc in same st and in each sc around;
join with slip st to first sc changing to Blue.

Rnd 11: Ch 1, sc in same st and in each sc around; join
with slip st to first sc changing to Dk Blue.

Rnds 12-16: Repeat Rnds 3-7.

Rnd 17: Ch 1, sc in same st and in next 2 sc, decrease,
(sc in next 3 sc, decrease) around; join with slip st to first
sc: 48 sc.

Rnd 18: Ch 1, sc in same st and in next sc, decrease,
(sc in next 2 sc, decrease) around; join with slip st to first
sc: 36 sc.

Rnd 19: Ch 1, sc in same st, decrease, (sc in next sc,
decrease) around; join with slip st to first sc: 24 sc.

Rnds 20 and 21: Repeat Rnds 18 and 19: 12 sc.

Rnd 22: Ch 1, pull up a loop in same st and in next
sc, YO and draw through all 3 loops on hook, decrease
around; join with slip st to first st, finish off leaving a long
end for sewing.

Thread yarn needle with yarn end and weave through sts
on Rnd 22; gather **tightly** and secure end.

Using both colors, make pom-pom *(Figs. 7a-c, page 2)*
and sew to top of Cap.

Turn bottom edge up as desired.